FAMILIES AROUND THE WORLD

A family from
SOUTH AFRICA

Jen Green

RSVP

RAINTREE
STECK-VAUGHN
P U B L I S H E R S
The Steck-Vaughn Company

Austin, Texas

FAMILIES AROUND THE WORLD

A family from **BOSNIA**

A family from **BRAZIL**

A family from **CHINA**

A family from **ETHIOPIA**

A family from **GERMANY**

A family from **GUATEMALA**

A family from **IRAQ**

A family from **JAPAN**

A family from **SOUTH AFRICA**

A family from **VIETNAM**

The family featured in this book is an average South African family.
The Qampies were chosen because they were typical of the majority of South
African families in terms of income, housing, number of children, and lifestyle.

Cover: The Qampies outside their home with all their possessions
Title page: Simon and Poppy walk home after a trip to the supermarket.
Contents page: A street vendor sells corn to people on their way to work.

Picture acknowledgments: All the photographs in this book were taken by Peter Menzel.
The photographs were supplied by Material World/Impact Photos and were first published by
Sierra Club Books in 1994 © Copyright Peter Menzel/Material World.
The map artwork on page 4 was produced by Peter Bull.

Published by Raintree Steck-Vaughn Publishers,
an imprint of Steck-Vaughn Company

Library of Congress Cataloging-in-Publication Data
Green, Jen.
A family from South Africa / Jen Green.
p. cm.—(Families around the world)
Includes bibliographical references and index.
ISBN 0-8172-4902-8
1. South Africa—Social life and customs—Juvenile literature.
2. Family life—Juvenile literature.
[1. Family life—Ethiopia. 2. Ethiopia.]
I. Title. II. Series: Families around the world.
DT1974.G74   1998
306.85'0968—dc21   97-10022

Printed in Italy. Bound in the United States.
1 2 3 4 5 6 7 8 9 0 02 01 00 99 98

Contents

Introduction

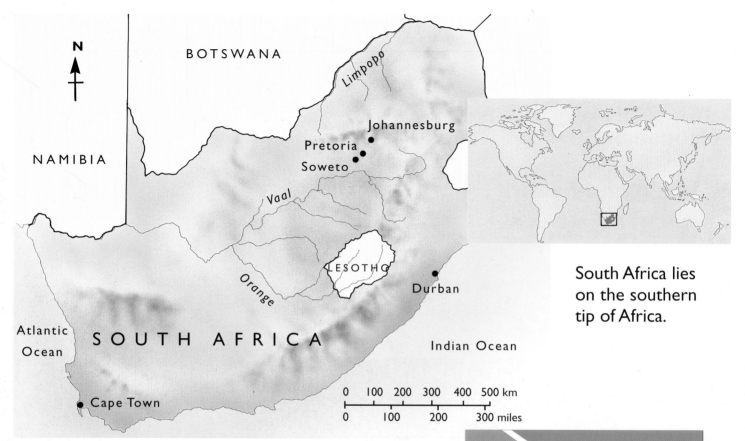

South Africa lies on the southern tip of Africa.

REPUBLIC OF SOUTH AFRICA

Capital city:	Pretoria
Size:	472,281 sq. mi. (1,221,040 sq. km.)
Number of people:	44,000,000
Languages:	11 official languages, including Xhosa, Zulu, Afrikaans, English, North Sotho, and Sesotho
Peoples:	Xhosa, Zulu, Swazi, Tswana, Afrikaner, British, Indian, people of mixed race, Sotho, and many other African peoples
Religion:	Mainly independent black churches, Afrikaans Reformed, Roman Catholic, and Methodist
Currency:	Rand

THE QAMPIE FAMILY

Size of household: eight

Size of home: 400 sq. ft. (37 sq. m.)

Workweek: Simon: 40 hours
Poppy: 40 hours

Most valued
possessions: Simon and Poppy: TV and radio
George and Matteo:
their tricycles

Family income: $2,543 each year

The Qampie family is an average South African family. The Qampies have put everything that they own outside their home so that this photograph could be taken.

Meet the Family

NEW SOUTH AFRICA

South Africa has changed a lot in the last few years. Until 1994 only white-skinned people had a say in how the country was run. Now everyone can vote. The country has a new government and a black president, Nelson Mandela.

1 Simon, father, 48
2 Poppy, mother, 36
3 Anna, Poppy's sister, 18
4 Irene, daughter, 11

5 George, son, 4
6 Pearl, daughter, 14
7 Matteo, Anna's son, 2
8 Leah, Poppy's mother, 64

In April 1994, Simon and Poppy Qampie became a part of South African history. Along with 19 million other South Africans, they voted in the first-ever real South African election. The Qampies voted alongside white, black, and Asian South Africans. This day was one they had waited for their whole lives.

"I love riding my tricycle around the yard. Sometimes Mom lets me ride on the street if I promise not to go too far."—*George*

A House in Soweto

The streets of Soweto have no names—the Qampies live at number 8838.

SOWETO

The name "Soweto" stands for South Western Townships. Soweto is a group of townships on the outskirts of Johannesburg. More than a million people live there. Soweto has no town center, but there are two swimming pools, two movie theaters, and a few small parks.

The Qampies' home is a small brick house. The house has gas and electricity and a faucet with cold water. The Qampies feel they are lucky. Many families in Soweto live in houses built from scrap wood and corrugated iron, without any water or electricity.

The Qampies rent their house. It has a kitchen, living room, and bedroom. The kitchen has a stove and a refrigerator. There is no shower, and the toilet is in a small shed in the backyard.

There is enough room in the kitchen for Poppy and Anna to sit and talk while the food is cooking.

Sleeping and Relaxing

The bedroom has two beds. Simon, Poppy, and Matteo sleep in one. Anna, Irene, and George share the second bed. Leah sleeps there when she stays overnight. Pearl does not sleep at home during the week. She lives with her aunt Judith in another township and goes to school there.

"When there are four of us, it's a bit of a squash in our bed. Sometimes there's not much room for me!"
—*George*

▲ Simon and Poppy like watching serials and the news on television. The children enjoy comedy programs best.

The living room is the most comfortable room in the house. A coal stove keeps the room warm in winter. Poppy has decorated the living room with ornaments and plants. She keeps her glass objects safe in a cabinet there.

Cooking and Eating

Most of the family's meals are cooked on this stove.

SPAZAS

Most families do their shopping at the local store. There are hundreds of these small shops in Soweto, selling everything from bread, salt, and sugar to paraffin for the stove.

Mealie with Everything

Corn meal, called "mealie" in South Africa, is the most important food for the Qampies. Mealie is mixed with water to make "pap," or porridge. It is cooked and served as part of every meal.

Most of the family's food is bought at the local store, or *spaza*. Simon and Poppy go there on Sundays and carry back the shopping. Poppy buys onions, tomatoes, pumpkins, and green vegetables at the local market.

Back home, Poppy unpacks everything
she has bought at the spaza.

Breakfast, Lunch, and Dinner

Breakfast is the children's favorite meal. Poppy gives them liverwurst (slices of sausage) to eat with corn meal cereal. The family eats breakfast early, so that the children are ready for school, and so that Simon and Poppy can be at work on time.

For lunch the children have pap with milk or rice with meat and vegetables. At dinnertime Poppy usually cooks pap and soup or the same food as they had at lunchtime. Sometimes the children complain when they have to eat the same thing for lunch and dinner!

Poppy feeds Matteo his cereal in the morning.

"I always start the day with porridge."
—*Leah*

At Work

In Soweto many people do not have jobs. Simon and Poppy are lucky to have full-time work.

Traveling to Work

Simon works as a security guard in a suburb of Johannesburg, 6 mi. (10 km.) from home. There are few jobs in Soweto, so almost everyone works in Johannesburg. Simon travels to work by train. It takes him about thirty minutes to get there. The journey to Johannesburg takes him past the high heaps of earth dug out long ago from the town's gold mines.

16

"I work at a department store. Sometimes it gets boring when things are very quiet."—*Simon*

One of Poppy's jobs is to take her company's money to the bank.

To the City

Poppy works as an office assistant at a computer training center. Her office is in the center of Johannesburg, about 10 mi. (15 km.) from Soweto. Poppy travels to work by minibus taxi. The minibuses drive very fast, racing one another to the city center.

Poppy arrives at work by 8:00 A.M. One of Poppy's main jobs is filing letters and papers. Soon after 4:00 P.M. she boards a minibus for the trip back to Soweto.

These people are waiting to catch the minibus taxi to work. It is a popular way to travel in Soweto.

At School

Irene has been going to school since she was five years old. George and Matteo can't wait to go to school.

South Africa's new government wants all children to go to school for at least ten years, until the age of 15 or 16. Many new schools are being built, but there are not enough teachers to go around.

Going to Nursery

On weekdays the children go to school. George and Matteo go to the local nursery, less than a mile from home. At the nursery George and Matteo are learning to read and write in English and in Xhosa, an African language. George is looking forward to being five, so that he can go to the local school, just like his sister Irene.

"Leah sometimes takes us to the nursery. I like going there. The helpers are kind and no one is strict."—*George*

Studying Hard

Pearl goes to school in a township near where Simon works. During the week she stays with an aunt who lives nearby. Pearl's school has little money. The buildings are made from containers, roofed with sheets of corrugated iron.

At Pearl's school, lessons start at 8:00 A.M. The children leave for home at 4:30 P.M.

"There are more than 40 pupils in my class. We haven't enough textbooks to go around, so we share them."—*Pearl*

At school Pearl learns in three different languages—Xhosa, English, and Afrikaans. She studies math, science, geography, history, and farming. Pearl spends eight hours in school every weekday except in December. This is midsummer in South Africa.

Spare Time

The Qampies have a television and a radio that they like to listen to when they have free time.

South Africa is famous for its youth choirs, made up of students and young people. Some choirs meet every day to practice, and they compete at talent competitions.

After School

Irene, George, and Matteo come home from school at 2:00 P.M. They like to play on the grass outside. Then Irene washes her school shirt. She hangs it out to dry so that it will be ready for the next day. Irene's homework takes an hour or two.

24

The children like to dance around in a circle. Sometimes Matteo gets dizzy!

Off to Church

In the evenings and on Sundays, the church bells of Soweto's large Roman Catholic church ring out. The whole family goes to church, and the children go to Sunday school.

"Religion is important in our family. We often pray and go to church."—*Irene*

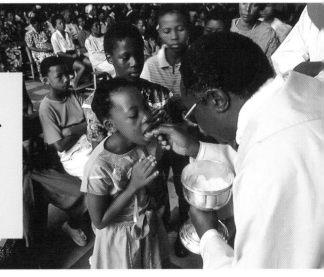

George joins in a game of checkers.
The counters are bottletops.

On Weekends

Weekends are busy for Simon and Poppy. There are many chores to be done before the family can relax! Simon and Poppy go to the supermarket. Then Poppy cleans the house and washes the clothes in a large basin.

Simon enjoys watching boxing and soccer games on television. At halftime, while the teams are resting, he rushes outside to cut the grass with shears. Later, Simon and Poppy listen to the radio.

"I like to keep the grass short, but it takes a long time to cut it with these shears!"—*Simon*

The Future

Simon would like to own a car. Poppy would like the family to own its own home. But for both Simon and Poppy, the children's schooling is the most important thing. With a good education, Simon and Poppy hope the young ones can have a better future when they grow up. Everyone hopes for better times in the new South Africa.

Simon and Poppy on the street near their house. One day they might buy their own home.

A PROMISE OF HOPE

South Africa's president, Nelson Mandela, has promised: "We shall build the society in which all South Africans, black and white, will be able to walk tall, without any fear in their hearts."

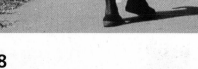

"I want to learn how to use a computer like the people in Mom's office when I grow up. My teacher says I'll have to study hard."—*Irene*

Pronunciation Guide

Afrikaans	Af-ri-kans
apartheid	A-part-hide
Johannesburg	Joe-hann-es-berg
Leah	Lee-ah
Lesotho	Leh-**sew**-toe
Mandela	Man-**dell**-ah
Matteo	Mah-**tay**-oh
Pretoria	Pri-**tor**-ee-uh

Qampie	**Kwam**-pee
Sesotho	Say-**sew**-toe
Sotho	So-toe
Soweto	So-**ay**-toe
spaza	spah-zah
Tswana	Swah-nuh
Xhosa	Zoh-sah

Glossary

Afrikaans The language of Afrikaners, people descended from South Africa's Dutch settlers.

Apartheid A set of laws that divided South Africans into racial groups. The word apartheid means "separateness" in Afrikaans.

Colony A settlement abroad controlled by the new settlers or by their home country's government.

Elections When people elect, or vote for, their country's government.

Government A group of people who run the country.

Outskirts The outer area of a town or city.

President The head of a country's government, elected by the people.

Roman Catholic Belonging to a worldwide religion headed by the Pope in Rome, Italy.

Suburb A built-up area on the edge of a town or city.

Townships Poor areas for black people, on the edges of towns in which white people live.

Xhosa An African people; also their language.

Books to Read

Flint, David. *South Africa*. Modern Industrial World. Austin, TX: Raintree Steck-Vaughn, 1997.

Lowis, Peter. *South Africa*. Topics in the News. Austin, TX: Raintree Steck-Vaughn, 1996.

Pogrund, Benjamin. *Nelson Mandela*. Milwaukee, WI: Gareth Stevens, 1993.

Rosmarin, Ike. *South Africa*. Tarrytown, NY: Marshall Cavendish, 1993.

Index